Sainsbury's

·RECIPE·LIBRARY·

# SALADS

Sainsbury's

·RECIPE·LIBRARY·

# SALADS

Mary Cadogan

# CONTENTS




Published exclusively for J Sainsbury plc
Stamford House Stamford Street London SE1 9LL
by Martin Books
Simon & Schuster Consumer Group
Fitzwilliam House 32 Trumpington Street
Cambridge CB2 1QY

ISBN 0 85941 530 9
First published 1986
Fourth impression 1991



Printed and bound in Italy by Arnoldo Mondadori Editore

# INTRODUCTION

A salad is a dish that is almost impossible to define. It is usually cold, but not always so—some of the most delicious salads are served warm. A salad is usually served as an accompaniment, but it can be a meal in itself. Oil and vinegar or mayonnaise are the most common dressings; avocado purée, fresh tomato pulp, blue cheese, yogurt and soured cream are just a few of the many interesting flavours you can use. A salad is often a combination of leaves—the first salads were simply freshly picked raw vegetables seasoned with salt—but it can just as often contain such diverse ingredients as nuts, dried fruits, sunflower seeds, kidney beans and pasta.

A common element in all successful salads is that the fresh ingredients are just that—morning-fresh and in peak condition. If you cannot buy fresh on the day, store for a short time in the refrigerator; this applies to root vegetables too if they are to be eaten raw. When shopping for salad ingredients, be adaptable and try to use produce in season. If the lettuce is limp, try Chinese leaves or young spinach; if the celery lacks crunch, go for carrots, beans or courgettes instead. Check avocados are ripe, lettuce is hearty, radishes are firm, and so on.

Always dry salad leaves carefully before adding them to the salad bowl. If too much water clings to the leaves it will dilute the dressing. A salad spinner is useful, but for leaves that bruise easily a clean teatowel is gentler. Leafy salads and those which contain tomatoes are best dressed just before serving.

When cooking vegetables for a salad, time the cooking carefully to ensure they are tender but retain a crunch. Vegetables like French beans, mangetouts and young broad beans need only brief blanching. Plunge the cooked vegetables in cold water to stop them cooking further and to preserve their colour.

A final word about presentation. Choose serving dishes to show off salads without detracting from them: glass, wood and white china are ideal, but there are no rules. Simply arrange your salads to look really appetizing.

NOTES

Ingredients are given in both metric and imperial measures. Use either set of quantities but not a mixture of both in any one recipe.

All spoon measurements are level:
1 tablespoon = one 15 ml spoon
1 teaspoon = one 5 ml spoon.

Fresh herbs are used unless otherwise stated. If unobtainable dried herbs can be substituted in cooked dishes but halve the quantities.

Freshly ground black pepper is intended where pepper is listed.

Eggs are standard size 3 unless otherwise stated.

Basic recipes are marked with an asterisk and given in the reference section (pages 76–79). Increase or decrease the basic quantities in proportion to obtain the amount required.

## SPINACH AND BACON SALAD

Raw spinach is sweet tasting and is a perfect complement to crispy bacon.

*175 g (6 oz) young spinach leaves, shredded*
*50 g (2 oz) button mushrooms, sliced*
*2 hard-boiled eggs, chopped*
*2 tablespoons oil*
*4 rashers streaky bacon, derinded and diced*
*2 tablespoons wine vinegar*
*pepper to taste*

**Serves 4**
**Preparation time:**
20 minutes

1. Divide the spinach between 4 individual serving bowls and sprinkle with the mushrooms and chopped egg.
2. Heat the oil in a frying pan, add the bacon and fry for about 6–8 minutes, until crisp and golden. Add the vinegar and pepper and bring to the boil. Pour over the individual salads and serve immediately.

## AVOCADO AND ORANGE SALAD

To check an avocado for ripeness, hold it in your hand; if it gives to gentle pressure, it is just right.

*2 large ripe avocados, halved, stoned and peeled*
*2 oranges*
*1 tablespoon roughly chopped walnuts*
*1 tablespoon olive oil*
*salt and pepper to taste*

**Serves 4**
**Preparation time:**
15 minutes

1. Place each avocado half, cut side down, on a small serving plate. Cut lengthways into thin slices, then press gently to fan out the slices on the plate.
2. Peel the oranges and divide into segments over a bowl to catch the juice, discarding all pith.
3. Arrange the orange segments beside the avocado slices and sprinkle with the walnuts.
4. Sprinkle the orange juice over the avocados, then drizzle over the oil. Season lightly with salt and pepper and serve immediately.

## CRAB-STUFFED ARTICHOKE HEARTS

These artichoke cups are a little fiddly to prepare, but make a pretty summer starter, when artichokes are cheap and plentiful. Use fresh or canned crab meat.

*4 globe artichokes*
*2 tablespoons lemon juice*
*4 lettuce leaves*
*4 teaspoons French Dressing**
*250 g (8 oz) crab meat*
*4 teaspoons Mayonnaise**
*4 teaspoons lumpfish caviar, preferably red*
*salt to taste*

**Serves 4**
**Preparation time:**
25 minutes
**Cooking time:**
25–30 minutes

1. Remove the outer leaves and stalks from the artichokes, using a stainless steel knife. Cut 2.5 cm (1 inch) from the top of each one, then peel the bases. Cook in boiling salted water for 25–30 minutes, until tender.
2. Drain the artichokes upside down on kitchen paper, then remove the chokes with a teaspoon and discard. Brush liberally with the lemon juice.
3. Place each artichoke cup on a lettuce leaf on a small plate. Spoon a teaspoon of dressing into each, then fill with crab meat. Top each with a teaspoonful of mayonnaise and lumpfish caviar to serve.

## GOAT'S CHEESE AND ENDIVE SALAD

Chill the chèvre or goat's cheese thoroughly before grilling to ensure it keeps its shape.

*25 g (1 oz) walnuts, chopped finely*
*25 g (1 oz) wholemeal breadcrumbs*
*4 slices goat's cheese, about 1 cm (½ inch) thick*
*1 curly endive*
*125 g (4 oz) button mushrooms*
*8 walnut halves*
*½ quantity Honey French Dressing**

**Serves 4**
**Preparation time:**
25 minutes

1. Mix together the chopped walnuts and breadcrumbs. Press this mixture onto the slices of goat's cheese to coat well. Chill until firm.
2. Arrange the endive, mushrooms and walnut halves on 4 small plates. Sprinkle a little dressing over each.
3. Place the cheese slices on an oiled baking sheet and place under a preheated moderate grill for 3–4 minutes. Carefully turn with a palette knife and grill the other side for 2–3 minutes. Place a slice of cheese on each salad and serve immediately.

## EGGS IN WATERCRESS MAYONNAISE

*1 bunch watercress*
*5 tablespoons Mayonnaise**
*1 tablespoon orange juice*
*8 hard-boiled eggs*
*salt and pepper to taste*
*TO GARNISH:*
*4 orange slices, quartered*

1. Set aside a few watercress sprigs. Plunge the rest into boiling salted water for 1 minute, drain and cool under running cold water. Drain well, pressing out as much water as possible.
2. Place the watercress, mayonnaise and orange juice in a blender or food processor and work until fairly smooth. Season with a little salt and pepper.
3. Place some watercress mayonnaise on each serving plate. Halve the eggs and place on the sauce, cut sides up. Garnish with the reserved watercress and orange.

**Serves 8 (or 4 as a main course)**
**Preparation time:** 20 minutes

# BEEF AND GHERKIN SALAD

To make radish roses, make small semi-circular cuts all around the radish to look like petals. Chill in iced water until the 'petals' open.

*250 g (8 oz) thinly sliced roast beef*
*1 red onion, chopped finely*
*7 gherkins*
*1 tablespoon chopped parsley*
*1 quantity French Dressing**
*2 teaspoons coarse-grain mustard*
*TO GARNISH:*
*continental lettuce*
*radish roses (see above)*

**Serves 4**
**Preparation time:** 15 minutes, plus marinating

1. Cut the beef into strips and place in a dish with the onion. Slice 3 gherkins and add to the dish with the parsley.
2. Mix the French dressing with the mustard and pour over the beef. Cover and leave to marinate for up to 2 hours.
3. Just before serving, line 4 small plates with lettuce leaves and place a quarter of the meat on each plate. Cut the remaining gherkins into fans and place one on each plate. Garnish with radish roses.

# HERBED SALMON SALAD

This summer recipe makes the most of fresh salmon when it is at its cheapest and most flavoursome.

*2 salmon steaks, each weighing 250 g (8 oz)*
*5 tablespoons chopped parsley*
*2 tablespoons chopped dill*
*1 tablespoon chopped tarragon*
*2 tablespoons lemon juice*
*½ cucumber, peeled and sliced thinly*
*4 crisp lettuce leaves*
*2 tablespoons Mayonnaise**
*salt and pepper to taste*
*dill and/or tarragon sprigs to garnish*

1. Place the salmon steaks on a large piece of foil and sprinkle with the herbs, rubbing them well in. Sprinkle with the lemon juice, salt and pepper and place in a baking dish.
2. Cook in a preheated oven, 190°C/375°F/Gas Mark 5, for 15 minutes, until tender. Leave to cool.
3. Arrange the cucumber on 4 small serving plates and cover with a lettuce leaf.
4. Flake the salmon into a bowl. Add the cooking juices and mayonnaise and mix carefully. Spoon the mixture on top of the lettuce. Garnish with dill and/or tarragon.

**Serves 4**
**Preparation time:** 25 minutes
**Cooking time:** 15 minutes

## CAESAR SALAD

This is one of my favourite salads and should definitely be served as a course on its own to appreciate the wonderful combination of flavours.

*5 anchovies*
*1 fat clove garlic*
*8 thin slices French bread*
*1 cos lettuce*
*25 g (1 oz) Parmesan cheese, grated*

*FOR THE DRESSING:*
*1 egg*
*2 tablespoons lemon juice*
*3 tablespoons olive oil*
*1 teaspoon Worcestershire sauce*
*salt and pepper to taste*

**Serves** 4
**Preparation time:** 20 minutes
**Cooking time:** 15 minutes

1. Mash together the anchovies, garlic and a little of the anchovy oil; a pestle and mortar is best for this job. Spread a little of this mixture over each slice of bread.
2. Place the bread slices, anchovy side up, on a baking sheet and bake in a preheated oven, 150°C/300°F/Gas Mark 2, for 15 minutes, until the bread is crisp. Cut each slice in half.
3. Tear the lettuce into large pieces and place in a salad bowl with the bread. Sprinkle with the cheese.
4. For the dressing, place the egg in a pan of simmering water for 50 seconds, then remove and crack into a small bowl, spooning out any set white from the shell. Add the remaining dressing ingredients and whisk with a fork until smooth.
5. Pour over the salad just before serving and toss lightly.

## PASTRAMI AND AVOCADO ROLLS

Pastrami is spiced brisket. Thin slices of rare roast beef can be used instead.

*2 large ripe avocados*
*12 slices pastrami*
*1 quantity Parsley and Onion Dressing**
*lettuce leaves to garnish*

**Serves** 4
**Preparation time:** 15 minutes

1. Peel, halve and stone the avocados. Cut each half into 3 slices.
2. Wrap a slice of pastrami around each avocado slice and arrange on individual serving plates.
3. Pour the dressing evenly over the rolls and garnish with lettuce leaves. Serve as soon as possible.

## PEAR AND BLUE CHEESE SALAD

*75 g (3 oz) blue Stilton or Roquefort cheese*
*½ quantity Mayonnaise**
*1 tablespoon wine vinegar*
*2 firm pears*
*1 tablespoon lemon juice*
*1 tablespoon chopped walnuts*
*curly endive and/or chicory to garnish*

**Serves 4**
**Preparation time:** 15 minutes

1. Crumble the cheese into a bowl, then beat in the mayonnaise and vinegar to make a thick sauce.
2. Peel the pears, cut in half and remove the cores with a teaspoon. Brush the pears with the lemon juice.
3. Place each pear half, cut side down, on a serving plate. Cut lengthways into thin slices, then press gently to fan out the slices on the plate.
4. Pour a little cheese sauce over each pear half and sprinkle with the walnuts. Garnish with endive and/or chicory to serve.

## GREEK-STYLE AUBERGINES

This salad keeps well—in fact, improves after a few days. Store it in a covered container in the refrigerator for up to a week.

*2 aubergines*
*150 ml (¼ pint) dry white wine*
*150 ml (¼ pint) water*
*6 tablespoons olive oil*
*2 tablespoons lemon juice*
*1 clove garlic, crushed*
*few parsley sprigs*
*1 celery stick, chopped*
*½ teaspoon chopped thyme*
*6 peppercorns*
*6 coriander seeds, bruised*
*salt to taste*
*coriander sprigs to garnish*

**Serves 4**
**Preparation time:** 30 minutes, plus standing time
**Cooking time:** 15 minutes

1. Cut the aubergines into 2.5 cm (1 inch) chunks. Place in a colander over a bowl and sprinkle liberally with salt. Place a plate on top and leave for 45 minutes to drain.
2. Meanwhile, place the remaining ingredients and 1 teaspoon salt in a pan, bring to the boil, then simmer for 15–20 minutes. Strain and return to the pan.
3. Rinse the aubergine pieces and pat dry with kitchen paper. Add to the pan, bring to the boil, then cover and simmer for 15 minutes, until the aubergine is tender.
4. Transfer to a serving bowl and leave to cool at room temperature. Garnish with coriander to serve.

## SALAD WITH AVOCADO DRESSING

*1 crisp lettuce, shredded*
*½ cucumber, peeled and sliced*
*3 tomatoes, sliced*
*125 g (4 oz) button mushrooms, sliced*
*50 g (2 oz) stuffed olives, sliced*
*1 quantity Avocado Dressing**

1. Place the lettuce in individual serving bowls and arrange the cucumber and tomato slices alternately in a layer over the top. Cover with the mushroom slices.
2. Reserve a few slices of stuffed olive. Scatter the remainder over the mushrooms.
3. Just before serving, spoon the dressing over the salad and garnish with the reserved olives.

**Serves 4**
**Preparation time:**
25 minutes

## SPICED RICE SALAD

*250 g (8 oz) long-grain rice*
*1 teaspoon each ground turmeric, cumin, curry powder and coriander*
*600 ml (1 pint) water*
*2 tablespoons wine vinegar*
*4 tablespoons sunflower oil*
*125 g (4 oz) peas, cooked*
*1 onion, chopped*
*2 carrots, grated*
*75 g (3 oz) sultanas*
*75 g (3 oz) unsalted peanut kernels, lightly roasted*
*salt to taste*

**Serves** 4
**Preparation time:** 15 minutes
**Freezing:** Recommended

1. Place the rice, spices and water in a pan, bring to the boil, then cover and simmer for 12–15 minutes, until the water is absorbed and the rice is tender.
2. Turn into a bowl and stir in the vinegar, oil and salt. Leave until cold.
3. Fluff up the rice gently with a fork, then stir in the peas, onion, carrot, sultanas and peanuts.
4. Transfer the rice salad to a large serving bowl or 4 individual ones. Serve with a crisp green salad or Spiced Tomato Salad (page 54).

## GARDEN SALAD

The vegetables chosen here are in season in the spring and summer; in winter you could use old potatoes, celeriac, beetroot, leeks and cauliflower.

*250 g (8 oz) courgettes*
*175 g (6 oz) carrots*
*175 g (6 oz) baby turnips*
*125 g (4 oz) young spinach leaves*
*500 g (1 lb) small new potatoes, boiled*
*500 g (1 lb) shelled broad beans, cooked*
*½ quantity Garlic French Dressing**
*2 tablespoons natural yogurt*

**Serves** 4
**Preparation time:** 20 minutes

1. Coarsely grate the courgettes, carrots and turnips.
2. Place the spinach leaves on 4 dinner plates and arrange all the vegetables in small piles on top.
3. Mix together the dressing and yogurt and drizzle over the salads just before serving.

## MALAYSIAN SALAD

*250 g (8 oz) white cabbage, shredded*
*125 g (4 oz) French beans, halved*
*2 carrots, cut into matchstick pieces*
*1/4 cucumber, cut into matchstick pieces*
*125 g (4 oz) bean sprouts*
*4 hard-boiled eggs, sliced*
*few coriander leaves to garnish*

*FOR THE SAUCE:*
*50 g (2 oz) desiccated coconut*
*300 ml (1/2 pint) boiling water*
*1 tablespoon oil*
*1 small onion, chopped finely*
*75 g (3 oz) crunchy peanut butter*
*1 teaspoon chilli powder*
*1 teaspoon brown sugar*
*1 tablespoon lime juice*

**Serves** 4
**Preparation time:** 40 minutes, plus soaking time

1. First, prepare the sauce. Soak the coconut in the water for 20 minutes, then strain through a sieve, reserving the liquid. (Use the coconut in cakes.)
2. Heat the oil in a pan, add the onion and fry until softened. Stir in the peanut butter, chilli powder, sugar and coconut liquid. Bring to the boil, then simmer for 5 minutes, until thickened. Remove from the heat and stir in the lime juice. Leave to cool.
3. Blanch the cabbage in boiling salted water for 1 minute, then drain and cool under running cold water.
4. Cook the beans and carrots for about 5 minutes, until just tender, then drain and cool.
5. Spread the cabbage, carrot and beans over a large serving platter or on 4 individual plates. Arrange the cucumber and bean sprouts on top and cover with overlapping egg slices.
6. Pour over the sauce and garnish with coriander.

## PIZZA SALAD

*500 g (1 lb) tomatoes, sliced*
*1 small onion, sliced thinly*
*1 clove garlic, chopped finely*
*1 green pepper, cored, seeded and sliced*
*4 canned artichoke hearts, drained and halved*
*25 g (1 oz) black olives*
*125 g (4 oz) Mozzarella cheese, sliced thinly*
*1 teaspoon chopped marjoram*
*1 teaspoon chopped basil*
*1/2 quantity French Dressing**
*1 tablespoon grated Parmesan cheese*

1. Arrange the tomato slices on individual serving plates and sprinkle with the onion and garlic.
2. Place the green pepper rings around the edge of the plates with the artichoke hearts, then put a pile of olives in the centre.
3. Lay the Mozzarella slices over the green pepper. Sprinkle the herbs evenly all over the salad.
4. Just before serving, drizzle the dressing over the salad, then sprinkle with the Parmesan cheese.

**Serves 4**
**Preparation time:** 25 minutes

## FETA CHEESE SALAD

Try to get the authentic Greek Feta cheese for this salad; other varieties tend to be excessively salty.

*½ Iceberg lettuce, shredded*
*few endive sprigs (optional)*
*¼ Spanish onion, sliced thinly*
*1 green pepper, cored, seeded and sliced thinly*
*½ bunch watercress*
*8 radishes, quartered*
*175 g (6 oz) Feta cheese, cubed*
*12 black olives*
*FOR THE DRESSING:*
*3 tablespoons olive oil*
*1 tablespoon tarragon vinegar*
*salt and pepper to taste*

**Serves 4**
**Preparation time:**
20 minutes

1. Arrange the lettuce, endive, if using, onion, green pepper, watercress and radishes on a large platter or in shallow bowls. Sprinkle with the cheese and olives.
2. Mix together the dressing ingredients and pour over the salad just before serving.

## PEPPERED PASTA SALAD

*175 g (6 oz) dried pasta shapes, e.g. twists, spirals*
*1 tablespoon oil*
*1 large green pepper*
*1 large red pepper*
*3 celery sticks, chopped*
*125 g (4 oz) mushrooms, sliced*
*FOR THE SAUCE:*
*1 clove garlic*
*1 tablespoon capers*
*25 g (1 oz) parsley sprigs*
*1 tablespoon wine vinegar*
*1 teaspoon Dijon mustard*
*6 tablespoons olive oil*
*salt and pepper to taste*
*TO GARNISH:*
*50 g (2 oz) walnuts, chopped roughly*

**Serves 4**
**Preparation time:**
20 minutes

1. Cook the pasta according to packet directions, drain and rinse under running cold water. Drain well, then turn into a large bowl. Stir in the oil.
2. Core, seed and cut the peppers into chunks. Add to the pasta with the celery and mushrooms; mix well.
3. For the sauce, place the garlic, capers and parsley in a blender or food processor and chop finely. Add the vinegar and mustard and blend again. With the machine running, pour in the oil in a steady stream until the sauce is well blended. Season with salt and pepper.
4. Pour the sauce over the pasta, mixing well. Serve the salad sprinkled with the walnuts.

# DANISH POTATO SALAD

How many this salad serves depends greatly on the occasion and appetites. Served with a couple of light salads it is a good main course for 4; on its own, it's a substantial snack for 3 people.

*750 g (1½ lb) potatoes, boiled*
*2 hard-boiled eggs, chopped*
*50 g (2 oz) gherkins, sliced*
*1 tablespoon chopped parsley to garnish*

*FOR THE DRESSING:*
*50 g (2 oz) Danish blue cheese, grated*
*5 tablespoons natural yogurt*
*1 teaspoon clear honey*
*salt and pepper to taste*

**Serves 3–4**
**Preparation time:** 20 minutes

1. Cut the potatoes into large chunks and mix with the eggs and gherkins.
2. Place the cheese, yogurt, honey, and salt and pepper in a small bowl and mix well; be sparing with the salt as the cheese is salty. Add to the potato mixture and stir gently until the ingredients are coated in dressing.
3. Transfer the salad to a serving dish and sprinkle with the chopped parsley to garnish.

# DUTCH CHEESE SALAD

Mature Gouda, with its distinctive black rind, is becoming more commonly available. It has a deeper, stronger flavour than the young Gouda, with the same creamy texture. Use either type for this salad.

*2 slices bread*
*4 tablespoons oil*
*2 teaspoons paprika*
*3 carrots*
*1 red pepper, cored and seeded*
*3 celery sticks*
*175 g (6 oz) Gouda cheese*
*250 g (8 oz) Chinese leaves, shredded*
*1 quantity Yogurt and Herb Dressing**

1. Cut the bread into small cubes. Heat the oil in a frying pan, add the bread and fry until crisp and golden. Sprinkle over the paprika and fry for 1 minute, turning the bread to coat it evenly in the paprika. Remove the croûtons, drain on kitchen paper and leave to cool.
2. Cut the carrots, red pepper, celery and cheese into thin strips.
3. Place the Chinese leaves in a serving bowl and cover with the carrot, celery, pepper and cheese strips.
4. Just before serving, drizzle over the dressing and sprinkle with the croûtons.

**Serves 4**
**Preparation time:**
25 minutes

## KASHA PARCELS

Kasha is, I think, a better name for bulgur cracked wheat, partially cooked whole wheat grains which are dried and cracked. It has a wonderfully nutty texture and needs no cooking—just a quick soak before using. The parcels can be made up and chilled for several hours before serving.

*175 g (6 oz) bulgur cracked wheat*
*1 onion, chopped finely*
*3 tablespoons each chopped parsley and mint*
*50 g (2 oz) cooked sweetcorn kernels*
*2 tomatoes, skinned and chopped finely*
*3 tablespoons lemon juice*
*3 tablespoons olive oil*
*8 large crisp lettuce leaves*
*salt and pepper to taste*
*mint sprigs or spinach leaves to garnish*

**Serves 4**
**Preparation time:**
30 minutes, plus soaking time

1. Place the cracked wheat in a bowl and pour over plenty of hot water. Leave to soak for 30 minutes; it will swell considerably. Drain well, pressing out as much liquid as possible.
2. Place the cracked wheat in a bowl with the onion, herbs, sweetcorn and tomatoes and stir thoroughly.
3. Drizzle over the lemon juice and olive oil, mixing well, and season with salt and pepper.
4. Place a heaped tablespoon of Kasha on each lettuce leaf, fold in the sides and roll up to enclose the filling.
5. Place the parcels in a shallow dish or on a large plate and garnish with mint or spinach leaves to serve.

## BEAN SALAD WITH TOMATO DRESSING

If you prefer to use dried beans and chick peas, use 125 g (4 oz) of each.

*432 g ($15\frac{1}{4}$ oz) can red kidney beans, drained*
*432 g ($15\frac{1}{4}$ oz) can chick peas, drained*
*50 g (2 oz) black olives, halved and stoned*
*125 g (4 oz) button mushrooms, sliced*
*1 onion, chopped finely*
*1 quantity Tomato Dressing**
*few snipped chives*

**Serves 4**
**Preparation time:**
25 minutes

1. Mix together the beans, peas, olives, mushrooms and onion. Add the dressing and stir together well.
2. Transfer to a serving dish and sprinkle with chives. Store for up to 2 days in the refrigerator.

## CHICKEN AND MANGETOUT SALAD

Take care to cook the mangetouts briefly to preserve their delicate taste. When fresh basil is not in season, omit it altogether rather than use the dried herb.

*125 g (4 oz) mangetouts, topped and tailed*
*250 g (8 oz) cooked chicken, shredded*
*1 quantity Tomato Dressing**
*1 tablespoon chopped basil*
*1 tablespoon pistachio nuts, chopped*
*salt to taste*

**Serves 4**
**Preparation time:** 20 minutes

1. Plunge the mangetouts into boiling salted water for 1 minute, then drain and cool quickly under running cold water.
2. Mix together the mangetouts, chicken, dressing and basil. Place in a serving dish and sprinkle with the pistachio nuts.

## CURRIED EGG SALAD WITH PRAWNS

*1 tablespoon oil*
*1 small onion, chopped finely*
*2 teaspoons curry powder*
*2 teaspoons apricot jam*
*2 teaspoons lemon juice*
*142 ml (5 fl oz) carton soured cream*
*1 bunch watercress*
*6 eggs, hard-boiled and sliced*
*125 g (4 oz) peeled prawns*
*paprika*
*salt to taste*

**Serves 4**
**Preparation time:** 25 minutes

1. Heat the oil in a small saucepan, add the onion and fry gently until softened. Stir in the curry powder and cook for 1 minute.
2. Remove from the heat and stir in the jam, lemon juice, soured cream and salt. Leave to cool.
3. Scatter the watercress over a shallow serving dish and arrange the sliced eggs over the top, reserving a few slices for garnish. Sprinkle with the prawns.
4. Spoon the curry dressing over the eggs. Arrange the remaining egg slices on top and sprinkle with paprika to taste.

## BEEF AND TONGUE SALAD

This salad benefits from being made several hours before required, to allow the meat to marinate in the dressing.

*175 g (6 oz) sliced roast beef*
*175 g (6 oz) sliced tongue*
*1 small onion, chopped*
*2 teaspoons capers*
*2 teaspoons chopped parsley*
*1 quantity French Dressing**

**Serves 4**
**Preparation time:** 10 minutes, plus marinating

1. Cut the beef and tongue into thin strips. Arrange on 4 plates and sprinkle with the onion, capers and parsley.
2. Pour the dressing over the meat and mix gently until well coated. Cover with clingfilm until ready to serve.

## TURKISH CHICKEN

Nuts are used throughout the Middle East to thicken and flavour sauces.

*1 chicken, weighing about 1.5 kg (3 lb)*
*1 onion, quartered*
*1 carrot, sliced*
*1 celery stick, chopped*
*1 bay leaf*
*6 peppercorns*
*50 g (2 oz) walnuts, chopped finely*
*25 g (1 oz) fresh breadcrumbs*
*lettuce leaves*
*2 tablespoons oil*
*1 teaspoon paprika*
*salt and pepper to taste*

**Serves 4–6**
**Preparation time:** 30 minutes
**Cooking time:** 1¼ hours

1. Place the chicken in a saucepan with the onion, carrot, celery, bay leaf, peppercorns and salt. Add water to come halfway up the chicken, bring to the boil, then cover and simmer for 1¼ hours, until tender.
2. Leave the chicken to cool slightly in the stock, then remove from the pan, strain the stock and set aside.
3. Remove the bones and cut the chicken into large pieces.
4. Place the walnuts, breadcrumbs and 150 ml (¼ pint) of the reserved stock in a food processor or blender and work to a fairly smooth paste. Add salt and pepper if necessary.
5. Line 4–6 serving plates with lettuce leaves. Arrange the chicken on top and spoon over the walnut sauce.
6. Mix together the oil and paprika and drizzle over the top. Serve at room temperature.

# ITALIAN TURKEY SALAD

An ideal salad to serve on Boxing Day.

*350 g (12 oz) cooked turkey*
*2 red peppers, cored and seeded*
*125 g (4 oz) fennel bulb*
*2 teaspoons lemon juice*
*50 g ($1\frac{3}{4}$ oz) can anchovy fillets in oil*

*FOR THE DRESSING:*
*2 tablespoons lemon juice*
*1 teaspoon clear honey*
*1 clove garlic, crushed*
*1 teaspoon dry mustard*
*5 tablespoons olive oil*
*salt and pepper to taste*
*TO GARNISH:*
*chopped fennel*

**Serves 4–6**
**Preparation time:** 25 minutes

1. Cut the turkey into strips. Cut the red peppers into fine strips. Cut the fennel into fine strips and toss in the lemon juice to prevent discoloration.
2. Arrange half the fennel on a serving platter, cover with half the red pepper, then half the turkey. Repeat the layers.
3. Drain the anchovies, reserving the oil. Cut each anchovy in half lengthways and arrange on the salad.
4. Place all the dressing ingredients in a bowl, add the reserved anchovy oil and whisk until well blended. Pour over the salad just before serving, garnished with fennel.

# MARINER'S SALAD

*5 tablespoons white wine*
*few parsley sprigs*
*1 clove garlic*
*125 g (4 oz) scallops*
*500 g (1 lb) fresh mussels*
*½ red pepper, cored, seeded and sliced thinly*
*125 g (4 oz) peeled prawns*
*2 teaspoons capers*
*½ quantity Garlic French Dressing**
*1 tablespoon chopped parsley*
*6 black olives*
*salt and pepper to taste*

1. Place the wine, parsley, garlic, and salt and pepper in a large pan. Bring to the boil, add the scallops, then cover and simmer for 5 minutes, until tender. Remove with a slotted spoon and drain on kitchen paper.
2. Bring the liquid to the boil again. Add the mussels, discarding any that have already opened. Cook over a high heat, shaking the pan, for about 5 minutes, until the shells have opened; discard any that do not open. Drain and leave to cool, then remove from their shells.
3. Mix together the scallops, mussels, red pepper, prawns and capers. Add the dressing and parsley and toss well.
4. Transfer to individual serving dishes and arrange the olives over the top.

**Serves 4**
**Preparation time:**
20 minutes
**Cooking time:**
12 minutes

## TUNA AND TOMATO SALAD

Use either new potatoes or waxy ones for this salad, which can be served as a starter for 6 people.

*350 g (12 oz) potatoes, boiled and sliced*
*250 g (8 oz) tomatoes, skinned and sliced*
*198 g (7 oz) can tuna, drained*
*1 clove garlic, crushed*
*1 teaspoon Dijon mustard*
*2 teaspoons lemon juice*
*2 teaspoons walnut oil*
*1 tablespoon sunflower oil*
*1 hard-boiled egg*
*salt and pepper to taste*

**Serves 4**
**Preparation time:**
30 minutes

1. Arrange the potato and tomato slices alternately around 4 plates. Break the tuna into chunks and arrange on top.
2. Place the garlic, mustard, lemon juice, oils, and salt and pepper in a screw-topped jar and shake well to blend. Pour over the salad.
3. Halve the egg and remove the yolk. Chop the white and sprinkle over the salad, then sieve the yolk over the top.

## CREOLE PRAWN SALAD

This salad of prawns in a spicy dressing looks really colourful on its bed of tomato rice.

*2 tomatoes, skinned and seeded*
*½ teaspoon chilli powder*
*2 teaspoons paprika*
*1 clove garlic, crushed*
*1 quantity Lemon French Dressing**
*350 g (12 oz) peeled prawns*
*½ each red and yellow pepper, cored, seeded and chopped*
*125 g (4 oz) button mushrooms, sliced*
*4 spring onions, chopped*
*1 teaspoon tomato purée*
*250 g (8 oz) long-grain rice, cooked and cooled*
*spring onions to garnish*

**Serves 4**
**Preparation time:**
30 minutes

1. Finely chop or purée the tomato flesh. Add the chilli powder, paprika, garlic and half the dressing.
2. Place the prawns, peppers, mushrooms and spring onions in a bowl, add the tomato mixture and toss well.
3. Blend the tomato purée into the remaining dressing, pour over the rice and mix well.
4. Arrange the rice around the edge of 4 serving plates and fill the centre with the prawn salad. Garnish with spring onions and serve with corn chips.

## DUCK AND BEETROOT SALAD

*500 g (1 lb) cooked beetroot, sliced*
*1 red onion, sliced thinly*
*25 g (1 oz) mushrooms, sliced thinly*
*½ orange*
*1 teaspoon soy sauce*
*2 teaspoons Dijon mustard*
*2 tablespoons sunflower oil*
*1 teaspoon wine vinegar*
*2 duck breasts, cooked and sliced thinly*
*salt and pepper to taste*
*watercress to garnish*

**Serves 4**
**Preparation time:**
30 minutes

1. Place the beetroot in individual serving dishes and sprinkle with the onion rings and mushrooms.
2. Pare 2 strips of rind from the orange, cut into thin strips and set aside.
3. Squeeze the orange and mix the juice with the soy sauce, mustard, oil, vinegar, and salt and pepper. Whisk with a fork until thickened.
4. Arrange the duck slices neatly over the beetroot and pour the dressing evenly over the top. Sprinkle with the orange rind and garnish with watercress.

## SMOKED TROUT SALAD

Smoked trout has a subtle taste and moist, succulent texture. Serve this dish as a substantial starter, or as a main course with tiny steamed potatoes.

*175 g (6 oz) carrots*
*125 g (4 oz) fennel bulb*
*shredded lettuce*
*3 tablespoons French Dressing**
*4 smoked trout fillets, about 75 g (3 oz) each*
*3 tablespoons Mayonnaise**
*1 tablespoon chopped tarragon*
*2 tablespoons snipped chives*
*1 lime*

**Serves 4**
**Preparation time:**
25 minutes

1. Cut the carrot and fennel into matchstick pieces. Line individual serving plates with shredded lettuce and sprinkle the carrot and fennel over the top. Moisten with the French dressing.
2. Place the smoked trout on the vegetables.
3. Mix together the mayonnaise, tarragon and chives. Halve the lime, squeeze the juice from one half and beat into the mayonnaise.
4. Spoon the mayonnaise over the trout. Slice the reserved lime and use to garnish the salad.

# HERRING AND POTATO SALAD

*4 pickled herrings*
*500 g (1 lb) potatoes, boiled and diced*
*1 small red dessert apple, chopped*
*125 g (4 oz) dill pickles (optional), sliced thinly*
*2 teaspoons coarse-grain mustard*
*142 ml (5 fl oz) carton soured cream*
*watercress or dill to garnish*

1. Slice the herrings diagonally into strips. Place in a bowl with the potato, apple and pickles if using, and mix well.
2. Stir the mustard into the soured cream, add to the salad and mix well. Transfer to individual serving dishes and garnish with watercress or dill.

**Serves 4–6**
**Preparation time:** 25 minutes

## PORK AND RED CABBAGE SALAD

*500 g (1 lb) red cabbage, shredded finely*
*2 celery sticks, chopped*
*2 carrots, grated*
*1 red dessert apple, cored and chopped*
*1 small onion, grated*
*175 g (6 oz) cold roast pork, chopped*
*FOR THE DRESSING:*
*1 teaspoon coriander seeds*
*142 ml (5 fl oz) carton soured cream*
*1 tablespoon wine vinegar*
*salt and pepper to taste*

**Serves 4–6**
**Preparation time:** 30 minutes

1. Mix together the salad ingredients in a large bowl.
2. Crush the coriander seeds in a pestle and mortar, or in a bowl with the back of a tablespoon. Mix with the soured cream, vinegar, and salt and pepper. Add to the salad and mix thoroughly. Serve with crusty bread.

## KOFTA AND ARTICHOKE HEART SALAD

*25 g (1 oz) white bread, crusts removed*
*500 g (1 lb) lean minced beef*
*1 teaspoon ground cinnamon*
*½ teaspoon ground cumin*
*½ teaspoon ground coriander*
*1 egg, beaten*
*400 g (14 oz) can artichoke hearts*
*½ quantity French Dressing**
*1 tablespoon natural yogurt*
*1 tablespoon chopped coriander*
*salt and pepper to taste*
*oil for shallow-frying*
*coriander sprigs to garnish*

**Serves 4**
**Preparation time:** 25 minutes
**Cooking time:** 10 minutes

1. Break up the bread and place in a small bowl with water to cover. Leave to soak for 5 minutes, then squeeze the bread with one hand to remove excess water.
2. Place the soaked bread in a bowl with the minced beef, spices, egg, and salt and pepper. Mix thoroughly with a fork, then shape the mixture into about 30 small balls.
3. Fry the meatballs in hot oil for about 10 minutes, turning, until evenly browned. Remove from the pan and drain on kitchen paper. Leave to cool.
4. Drain the artichoke hearts, rinse under running cold water and dry with kitchen paper. Cut them in half and place in a bowl with the meatballs.
5. Combine the dressing, yogurt and chopped coriander, add to the salad and mix well. Transfer to a serving dish and garnish with coriander.

## CHICKEN RICE SALAD

*250 g (8 oz) long-grain rice*
*600 ml (1 pint) water*
*2 teaspoons paprika*
*1 tablespoon oil*
*1 tablespoon lemon juice*
*250 g (8 oz) cooked chicken meat*
*2 shallots, chopped finely*
*125 g (4 oz) button mushrooms, sliced*
*1 red pepper, cored, seeded and sliced thinly*
*300 ml (½ pint) Garlic Mayonnaise**
*salt and pepper to taste*
*mustard and cress to garnish*

**Serves 4–6**
**Preparation time:** 30 minutes

1. Place the rice, water and paprika in a pan, bring to the boil, then cover and simmer for 12–15 minutes, until the water has been absorbed and the rice is tender; drain thoroughly.
2. Place the rice in a bowl, add the oil and lemon juice and mix lightly. Leave to cool.
3. Chop the chicken into large pieces and add to the rice with the shallots, mushrooms and red pepper. Add the garlic mayonnaise and mix thoroughly. Season with salt and pepper.
4. Pile the salad into a serving bowl and garnish with mustard and cress.

## SALMON RICE RING

The pink and green flecks in this delicate rice salad make it attractive enough to show off to guests, yet it is economical enough for an everyday meal.

*250 g (8 oz) long-grain rice*
*600 ml (1 pint) fish or chicken stock*
*250 g (8 oz) tomatoes, skinned and chopped finely*
*8 stuffed olives, chopped finely*
*1 tablespoon snipped chives*
*1 tablespoon chopped parsley*
*2 tablespoons lemon juice*
*4 tablespoons olive oil*
*212 g (7½ oz) can pink salmon, drained and flaked*
*salt and pepper to taste*
*TO GARNISH:*
*2 carrots, sliced*
*curly endive*

1. Lightly oil a 23 cm (9 inch) ring mould.
2. Place the rice and stock in a saucepan, bring to the boil, then cover and simmer for 12 minutes, until tender.

3. Place the tomatoes and olives in a large bowl with the herbs, lemon juice and oil. Mix well, then add the warm rice. Stir carefully to distribute the ingredients evenly. Add the salmon, and salt and pepper.
4. Press the salad into the prepared ring mould, cover with clingfilm and chill for 2–3 hours.
5. Invert the salad onto a large serving plate and shake to remove it from the mould. Cut the carrot slices to make carrot 'flowers'. Garnish the salad with the carrot 'flowers' and endive.

**Serves 4–6**
**Preparation time:** 40 minutes

## PRAWN-STUFFED EGGS

This dish also makes a nice starter: allow one egg per person and reduce the other ingredients in proportion.

*8 hard-boiled eggs*
*175 g (6 oz) peeled prawns*
*3 tablespoons Mayonnaise**
*½ teaspoon chilli sauce*
*1 tablespoon tomato ketchup*
*shredded lettuce*
*½ bunch watercress*
*salt and pepper to taste*

**Serves 4**
**Preparation time:**
25 minutes

1. Halve the eggs, remove the yolks and sieve into a bowl. Finely chop the prawns and add to the yolks with the mayonnaise; mix well.
2. Add the chilli sauce and ketchup to the prawn mixture, then season with salt and pepper.
3. Arrange the lettuce and watercress on a large plate to make a 'nest'.
4. Sandwich the egg whites together with the prawn mixture, pressing into the hollow, and place in the centre of the plate.

## POTATO AND SALAMI LOAF

Use floury potatoes for this moulded salad, as they hold together well in the loaf and absorb plenty of dressing.

*1 kg (2 lb) potatoes*
*3 tablespoons Mayonnaise**
*½ quantity French Dressing**
*½ teaspoon celery seeds*
*175 g (6 oz) salami, sliced thinly*
*pepper to taste*
*lettuce leaves to garnish*

**Serves 4–6**
**Preparation time:**
45 minutes, plus chilling time

1. Cut the potatoes into small cubes and steam or boil until just tender; drain well.
2. While the potatoes are still warm, mix in the mayonnaise and dressing. Add the celery seeds and pepper and mix well.
3. Line a 1.2 litre (2 pint) loaf tin with overlapping slices of salami; reserve enough to cover the top. Press the potato salad into the tin and level the top with the back of a spoon. Cover with the reserved salami.
4. Cover with clingfilm and chill for several hours, until firm.
5. Invert the salad onto a serving plate and garnish with lettuce leaves. Slice the loaf thickly to serve.

## APPLE RICE SALAD

*250 g (8 oz) brown rice*
*300 ml (½ pint) apple juice*
*300 ml (½ pint) water*
*125 g (4 oz) cooked sweetcorn kernels*
*125 g (4 oz) small courgettes, grated*
*1 peach, chopped*
*50 g (2 oz) cashew nuts*
*1 quantity Lemon and Honey Dressing**
*3 tablespoons natural yogurt*
*salt and pepper to taste*

**Serves 4–6**
**Preparation time:**
45 minutes

1. Place the rice in a saucepan with the apple juice and water. Bring to the boil, then cover and simmer for 30–35 minutes, until the liquid is absorbed and the rice is tender. Transfer to a serving bowl and leave to cool slightly.
2. Mix in the sweetcorn, courgette, peach and nuts. Drizzle over the dressing and yogurt and mix lightly. Season with salt and pepper.

## PEPPERED HAM AND TOMATO SALAD

*175 g (6 oz) cooked ham, sliced thickly*
*250 g (8 oz) French beans, lightly cooked*
*2 teaspoons green peppercorns*
*350 g (12 oz) ripe tomatoes, skinned*
*1 teaspoon olive oil*
*1 tablespoon lemon juice*
*1 clove garlic, crushed*
*1 teaspoon clear honey*
*salt to taste*

**Serves 4**
**Preparation time:**
30 minutes

1. Cut the ham into cubes and the beans into 2.5 cm (1 inch) lengths. Mix together in a bowl.
2. Crush the peppercorns using a pestle and mortar or with the back of a spoon.
3. Cut each tomato into 8 wedges and place in a bowl with the peppercorns and remaining ingredients. Leave this mixture to stand for a few minutes, if possible.
4. Fold the tomato mixture into the ham and French beans to serve.

## EGG AND CUCUMBER SALAD

*1 cucumber, peeled and sliced thinly*
*½ bunch watercress*
*4 hard-boiled eggs*
*3 tablespoons natural yogurt*
*1 tablespoon chopped mint*
*salt and pepper to taste*

**Serves 2 (or 4 as a starter)**
**Preparation time:**
15 minutes

1. Mix together the cucumber and watercress and divide between individual serving plates.
2. Separate the egg whites and yolks. Chop the whites and half the yolks and sprinkle over the salad.
3. Mix together the yogurt, mint, and salt and pepper and pour over the salad. Sieve the remaining egg yolks over the top.

## SPICED CHICKEN SALAD

The chicken stays moist and full of flavour when cooked in a yogurt marinade.

*500 g (1 lb) boneless chicken breasts, skinned*
*1 small onion, chopped finely*
*150 g (5.3 oz) carton natural yogurt*
*1 teaspoon ground coriander*
*1 teaspoon curry powder*
*1 teaspoon paprika*
*½ teaspoon chilli powder*
*salt to taste*
*TO SERVE:*
*½ lettuce, shredded*
*½ cucumber, sliced*
*3 tomatoes, sliced*
*1 onion, sliced*
*1 tablespoon lemon juice*
*coriander leaves or parsley sprigs to garnish*

**Serves 4–6**
**Preparation time:**
20 minutes
**Cooking time:**
25–30 minutes

1. Place the chicken in a bowl. Mix together the onion, yogurt, spices and salt until well blended. (This can be done in a food processor or blender.) Pour over the chicken and leave to marinate for about 1 hour.
2. Remove the chicken from the marinade and place under a preheated moderate grill. Cook for about 25–30 minutes, basting with the marinade and turning occasionally. Leave to cool.
3. Line individual serving dishes with the lettuce and arrange the cucumber, tomatoes and onion over the top. Sprinkle with the lemon juice.
4. Cut the chicken into cubes and place on top of the salad. Garnish with coriander or parsley to serve.

## HERRING WITH ANCHOVIES

*4 pickled herrings*
*sorrel or dandelion leaves*
*350 g (12 oz) new potatoes, boiled and sliced thinly*
*2 tablespoons soured cream*
*2 anchovy fillets*
*8 capers*

1. Slice the herrings into thin diagonal strips.
2. Place 3 or 4 sorrel or dandelion leaves on 4 serving plates. Arrange the potato slices overlapping beside them.
3. On each plate place a criss-cross of herring strips over the potato and top with a little soured cream.
4. Cut each anchovy in half lengthways and place on the soured cream. Place 2 capers on top of each serving.

**Serves 4**
**Preparation time:** 20 minutes

## CHEESE AND FRUIT SALAD

*250 g (8 oz) Edam cheese, cubed*
*2 celery sticks, chopped*
*1 red dessert apple, chopped*
*125 g (4 oz) black grapes, halved and seeded*
*1 quantity Yogurt and Herb Dressing**

**Serves 4**
**Preparation time:**
15 minutes

1. Place the cheese in a bowl with the celery, apple and grapes.
2. Stir in the dressing and transfer to individual serving dishes. Serve with warm bread.

## CAERPHILLY AND BEETROOT SALAD

*175 g (6 oz) cooked beetroot, sliced thinly*
*125 g (4 oz) carrots, grated*
*175 g (6 oz) Caerphilly cheese, crumbled*
*4 teaspoons apple sauce*
*4 teaspoons low-calorie mayonnaise*
*salt and pepper to taste*
*2 spring onions, shredded*

**Serves 4**
**Preparation time:**
15 minutes

1. Arrange the beetroot slices on 4 small plates. Sprinkle with the carrot, then the cheese.
2. Mix together the apple sauce, mayonnaise, and salt and pepper and spoon a little over each salad. Sprinkle some shredded spring onion over the top.

## WENSLEYDALE SALAD

*500 g (1 lb) white cabbage, shredded finely*
*1 red pepper, cored, seeded and sliced thinly*
*175 g (6 oz) Wensleydale cheese, crumbled*
*6 spring onions, sliced thinly*
*8 black olives*
*FOR THE DRESSING:*
*4 tablespoons natural yogurt*
*1 teaspoon coarse-grain mustard*
*1 teaspoon clear honey*
*salt and pepper to taste*

**Serves 4**
**Preparation time:**
20 minutes

1. Spread the cabbage evenly over individual serving dishes and arrange the pepper strips on top. Sprinkle with the cheese, then the onions, then the olives.
2. Place the dressing ingredients in a small bowl and mix with a fork until well blended.
3. Just before serving, drizzle the dressing over the salad.

## MEXICAN POTATO SALAD

When in season, use tiny new potatoes for this salad and cook them whole.

*750 g (1½ lb) potatoes*
*1 onion, chopped roughly*
*1 clove garlic*
*1 tablespoon lemon juice*
*1 tablespoon tomato purée*
*1 tablespoon sherry*
*1 teaspoon clear honey*
*2 tablespoons natural yogurt*
*few drops Tabasco*
*salt to taste*
*1 tablespoon chopped parsley*

**Serves** 4–6
**Preparation time:** 20 minutes

1. Cut the potatoes into large chunks, or leave them whole if they are small. Steam or boil them until tender, drain and leave to cool.
2. Purée the onion and garlic in a blender or food processor. Add the lemon juice, tomato purée, sherry, honey, yogurt and Tabasco and work until smooth. Season with salt if necessary.
3. Place the potatoes in a serving dish. Spoon the dressing over the potatoes and sprinkle with the parsley.

## TURKEY AND CRANBERRY SALAD

This salad makes use of some of the ingredients you may have left over after a turkey dinner. You could add a few lightly cooked sliced vegetables too, such as carrots, potato or celery.

*300–350 g (10–12 oz) cooked turkey*
*4 spring onions*
*125 g (4 oz) radishes, sliced*
*125 g (4 oz) mushrooms, sliced*
*1 tablespoon cranberry sauce*
*1 quantity Yogurt and Herb Dressing**
*few lettuce leaves, shredded*
*few broken walnuts or chestnuts (optional)*

**Serves** 4
**Preparation time:** 20 minutes

1. Cut the turkey meat into chunks. Cut the spring onions into 5 cm (2 inch) lengths, then shred lengthways.
2. Place the turkey, spring onions, radishes and mushrooms in a bowl and mix well.
3. Stir the cranberry sauce into the dressing, then add to the turkey mixture, stirring well.
4. Line a serving platter with lettuce, pile the salad on top and sprinkle with walnuts or chestnuts if using.

## SLIMMER'S SALAD

If you are unable to obtain flavoured low-fat cheese, buy the plain variety and add 1 crushed clove garlic and 1 tablespoon chopped parsley.

*227 g (8 oz) packet low-fat soft cheese with garlic and herbs*
*1 tablespoon lemon juice*
*125 g (4 oz) carrot, grated*
*2 celery sticks, chopped finely*
*6 radishes, chopped finely*
*8–10 crisp lettuce leaves*
*salt and pepper to taste*
*radish slices to garnish*

1. Beat the cheese and lemon juice together in a bowl until softened. Add the carrot, celery and radishes and mix well. Season with salt and pepper if necessary.
2. Pile a little of the mixture onto each lettuce leaf and garnish with radish slices.

**Serves 4**
**Preparation time:**
15 minutes

## SMOKED MACKEREL SALAD

The slightly bitter tang of chicory and radicchio is the perfect foil for the rich flavour of smoked mackerel.

*250 g (8 oz) chicory*
*2 teaspoons lemon juice*
*125 g (4 oz) radicchio*
*350 g (12 oz) smoked mackerel*
*FOR THE DRESSING:*
*10 green peppercorns*
*3 tablespoons orange juice*
*4 teaspoons lemon juice*
*1 tablespoon snipped chives*
*1 teaspoon olive oil*
*salt and pepper to taste*

**Serves 4–6**
**Preparation time:** 20 minutes, plus standing time

1. Shred the chicory finely and toss in the lemon juice. Shred the radicchio and mix with the chicory. Spread over a serving platter or individual plates.
2. Skin and flake the mackerel and arrange on the salad.
3. Crush the peppercorns with a pestle and mortar, or in a bowl with the back of a tablespoon, and mix with the other dressing ingredients. If possible, leave the dressing to stand for 30 minutes to allow the flavours to develop.
4. Pour over the salad to serve.

# ST CLEMENT'S SOLE

*1 tablespoon white wine vinegar*
*1 bay leaf*
*few celery leaves*
*few peppercorns*
*4 sole fillets*
*2 oranges*
*juice of 1 lemon*
*125 ml (4 fl oz) dry white wine*
*4 spring onions, sliced thinly*
*salt and white pepper to taste*

1. Pour water into a large pan to a depth of 2.5 cm (1 inch). Add the vinegar, bay leaf, celery leaves and peppercorns, bring to the boil, then reduce to a simmer.
2. Add the sole, cover and cook for 5–6 minutes, until tender. Carefully remove from the pan and drain on kitchen paper. Leave to cool.
3. Thinly pare a strip of rind from 1 orange and chop finely. Squeeze the juice from both oranges.
4. Place the orange rind, orange and lemon juice, wine, spring onions, and salt and pepper in a large shallow bowl. Add the fish, cover with clingfilm and leave in the refrigerator overnight, or for at least 6 hours.
5. Serve the fish with a little of the marinade poured over.

**Serves 4**
**Preparation time:** 20 minutes, plus marinating
**Cooking time:** 5 minutes

## SPINACH AND APPLE SALAD

Use only young tender spinach leaves for this salad as these are the sweetest and most succulent.

*250 g (8 oz) spinach, shredded*
*1 red dessert apple, chopped*
*1 tablespoon sunflower seeds, toasted*
*1 tablespoon sesame seeds, toasted*
*25 g (1 oz) walnuts, chopped*
*FOR THE DRESSING:*
*1 tablespoon tarragon vinegar*
*3 tablespoons walnut oil*
*1 teaspoon Dijon mustard*
*salt and pepper to taste*

**Serves** 4–6
**Preparation time:**
20 minutes

1. Place all the salad ingredients in a serving bowl.
2. Place the dressing ingredients in a screw-topped jar and shake well to mix. Pour over the salad and toss lightly just before serving.

## BEAN AND MUSHROOM SALAD

*250 g (8 oz) French beans, cut into 2.5 cm (1 inch) lengths*
*125 g (4 oz) button mushrooms, sliced*
*1 teaspoon curry powder*
*1 tablespoon wine vinegar*
*2 tablespoons oil*
*1 tablespoon Mayonnaise**
*salt and pepper to taste*
*25 g (1 oz) flaked almonds, toasted, to garnish*

**Serves** 4
**Preparation time:**
15 minutes

1. Cook the beans in boiling salted water for 5–8 minutes, until just tender. Drain and cool under running cold water. Place in a bowl, add the mushrooms and mix well.
2. Place the curry powder, vinegar and oil in a small bowl and mix with a fork until smooth. Blend in the mayonnaise, and salt and pepper.
3. Pour the dressing over the salad and toss lightly.
4. Transfer to a serving bowl and sprinkle with the almonds to serve.

## ANDALUSIAN SALAD

The traditional ingredients for Gazpacho are here cut into chunks and moistened with a garlic-laced tomato dressing. If you can't get passata, use sieved canned tomatoes instead.

*175 g (6 oz) small courgettes*
*1 green pepper, cored and seeded*
*1 red pepper, cored and seeded*
*1 onion*
*½ cucumber*

*FOR THE DRESSING:*
*5 tablespoons passata*
*2 cloves garlic, crushed*
*2 tablespoons olive oil*
*1 tablespoon wine vinegar*
*salt and pepper to taste*
*TO GARNISH:*
*few flaked almonds*

Serves 4
**Preparation time:**
25 minutes, plus chilling time

1. Cut all the vegetables into even-size dice, place in a bowl and mix together well.
2. Whisk the dressing ingredients together and stir into the vegetables. Cover with clingfilm and chill for 1 hour, stirring occasionally.
3. Transfer to a serving dish and sprinkle with flaked almonds.

## SPICED TOMATO SALAD

This salad has a wonderfully cooling effect when eaten with spicy food, but it's also good with any cold meats.

*250 g (8 oz) tomatoes, skinned and chopped*
*grated rind and juice of 1 lemon*
*¼ teaspoon ground black pepper*
*¼ teaspoon chilli powder*
*½ teaspoon turmeric*
*1 small onion, chopped finely*
*2.5 cm (1 inch) piece fresh root ginger, grated finely*
*few coriander leaves to garnish (optional)*

Serves 4
**Preparation time:**
15 minutes, plus chilling time

1. Place the tomatoes, lemon rind and juice in a bowl and mix well.
2. Combine the remaining ingredients in a small bowl. Sprinkle over the tomatoes, mixing well. Cover with clingfilm and chill for 1 hour.
3. Just before serving, give the mixture a final stir and sprinkle with coriander, if wished.

## SUMMER GREEN SALAD

This is one of those 'flexible' salads, into which you can throw any leaves you have available—the following is merely a suggestion.

*½ Cos or Webbs lettuce*
*½ oak leaf lettuce*
*few dandelion or sorrel leaves*
*few young spinach leaves or corn salad*
*1 quantity Lemon French Dressing**
*2 tablespoons chopped mixed herbs, e.g. mint, chervil, tarragon, marjoram*

1. Roughly tear the leaves and place in a bowl. Mix together lightly with the fingers.
2. Pour over the dressing just before serving, toss lightly and sprinkle with the herbs.

**Serves 4**
**Preparation time:** 10 minutes

## TOMATO AND BASIL SALAD

*500 g (1 lb) tomatoes, sliced*
*8 basil leaves, chopped*
*1 tablespoon pine nuts*
*1 tablespoon olive oil*
*salt and pepper to taste*
*basil leaves to garnish*

**Serves 4**
**Preparation time:**
10 minutes

1. Arrange the tomatoes on individual serving plates and sprinkle with the basil and pine nuts.
2. Just before serving, drizzle the oil over the tomatoes and season with salt and pepper. Garnish with basil.

## BEAN SPROUT SALAD

Use canned or cooked frozen sweetcorn for this salad.

*175 g (6 oz) bean sprouts*
*125 g (4 oz) button mushrooms, sliced*
*75 g (3 oz) cooked sweetcorn kernels*
*1 red pepper, cored, seeded and diced*
*1 quantity French Dressing**
*3 thick spring onions, cut into matchstick shreds*

**Serves 4–6**
**Preparation time:**
10 minutes

1. Place the bean sprouts, mushrooms, sweetcorn and red pepper in a bowl and mix together well.
2. Just before serving, pour over the dressing and toss lightly. Transfer to individual serving dishes and sprinkle with the spring onions.

## THREE PEPPER SALAD

The assorted peppers make this a fairly dazzling salad. It is very rich so although the quantities seem small, a little is sufficient. It will keep for up to 3 days in the refrigerator. Use at least 2 cloves garlic in the dressing.

*3 large peppers, one each of red, green and yellow*
*½ quantity Garlic French Dressing**

**Serves 4**
**Preparation time:**
20 minutes

1. Place the whole peppers under a fairly hot grill until the skin is charred, turning them frequently.
2. Remove from the heat and cool slightly, then peel off the skins. Cut off the tops and remove the seeds.
3. Cut the peppers lengthways into strips and place in a bowl. Pour over the dressing. Toss well to serve.

## CUCUMBER SALAD

*1 cucumber, peeled and cut into chunks*
*2 tablespoons chopped dill, or 2 teaspoons dried dill*
*4 tablespoons soured cream*
*2 teaspoons white wine vinegar*
*salt and pepper to taste*
*dill sprig to garnish (optional)*

**Serves 4**
**Preparation time:** 10 minutes, plus soaking and chilling time

1. Place the cucumber in a sieve or colander over a bowl and sprinkle with salt. Leave for 1 hour to drain. Rinse well, drain and pat dry with kitchen paper, then place in a bowl and stir in the dill.
2. Mix together the soured cream, vinegar, and salt and pepper. Pour over the cucumber and chill for 30 minutes.
3. Stir well, then turn into a serving dish. Garnish with dill, if liked.

## FATTOUSH

This Middle Eastern salad is based on bread. The herby dressing is absorbed by the bread, giving it a deliciously tangy flavour.

*½ cucumber, chopped*
*8 slices French bread, 1 cm (½ inch) thick*
*3 tomatoes, skinned and chopped*
*1 onion, chopped finely*
*2 tablespoons chopped parsley*
*1 tablespoon chopped mint*
*1 clove garlic, crushed*
*1 quantity Lemon French Dressing**
*salt to taste*

**Serves 4**
**Preparation time:** 15 minutes, plus standing time

1. Place the cucumber in a colander and sprinkle with salt. Leave to drain for 30 minutes, then rinse well and dry with kitchen paper.
2. Toast the bread on both sides, until brown and crispy. Cut into small pieces.
3. Place the tomatoes, onion and cucumber in a bowl and mix well.
4. Add the herbs and garlic to the dressing and mix well.
5. Just before serving, add the bread and dressing to the vegetables. Stir well, then transfer to a serving dish.

# COURGETTE AND TARRAGON SALAD

Raw courgettes have a sweet taste; combined with a little tarragon they make an interesting side salad. Do not dress the courgettes until just before serving.

*500 g (1 lb) young courgettes, grated coarsely*

*2 teaspoons chopped tarragon*

*½ quantity Lemon French Dressing**

1. Place the courgettes in a serving dish and sprinkle with the tarragon, mixing gently.
2. Just before serving, pour over the dressing.

**Serves 4**
**Preparation time:** 15 minutes

## WINTER GREEN SALAD

The following salad leaves are at their best in winter. If you are not able to get walnut oil, use more olive oil instead.

*1/4–1/2 Iceberg lettuce, shredded*
*handful curly endive*
*1 head chicory*
*1/2 bunch watercress*
*1 tablespoon wine vinegar*
*1 teaspoon Dijon mustard*
*2 tablespoons olive oil*
*1 tablespoon walnut oil*
*salt and pepper to taste*

**Serves** 4
**Preparation time:** 10 minutes

1. Place the lettuce and endive in a salad bowl. Separate and slice the chicory leaves, then add to the salad with the watercress.
2. Place the remaining ingredients in a screw-topped jar and shake well to mix.
3. Toss the salad in the dressing just before serving.

## HOT DRESSED VEGETABLES

This way of serving hot vegetables, with a light dressing, is a favourite with Italians. Choose any selection of vegetables that can be cooked together.

*500 g (1 lb) leeks, cut into 2.5 cm (1 inch) lengths*
*1 small cauliflower, broken into florets*
*250 g (8 oz) carrots, sliced*
*4 celery sticks, sliced*
*2 tablespoons lemon juice*
*6 tablespoons olive oil*
*salt and pepper to taste*

**Serves** 4–6
**Preparation time:** 15 minutes
**Cooking time:** 6–8 minutes

1. Boil or steam the vegetables for 6–8 minutes, until just tender.
2. Whisk together the lemon juice, oil, and salt and pepper in a bowl.
3. Drain the vegetables and place in a warmed serving dish. Pour over the dressing and serve.

## SUNFLOWER CABBAGE SALAD

*350 g (12 oz) firm white or red cabbage, or a mixture, shredded*
*175 g (6 oz) carrots, grated coarsely*
*½ red pepper, cored, seeded and chopped*
*1 small onion, chopped finely*
*25 g (1 oz) sunflower seeds*
*50 g (2 oz) chopped dates*
*2 tablespoons Mayonnaise**
*1 tablespoon wine vinegar*
*1 teaspoon Dijon mustard*
*2 tablespoons sunflower oil*
*salt and pepper to taste*

**Serves 6–8**
**Preparation time:**
20 minutes

1. Place the cabbage, carrot, red pepper, onion, sunflower seeds and dates in a salad bowl and mix well.
2. Whisk the remaining ingredients together until smooth, pour over the salad and toss well to mix. Serve within a few hours.

## GINGERED CARROT AND RAISIN SALAD

*500 g (1 lb) carrots, grated coarsely*
*75 g (3 oz) raisins*
*½ teaspoon grated fresh root ginger*
*1 quantity Lemon French Dressing**
*1 tablespoon snipped chives or spring onion tops*

**Serves 4**
**Preparation time:**
15 minutes

1. Place the carrot and raisins in a bowl and mix well.
2. Add the ginger to the dressing and pour over the carrot mixture just before serving. Transfer to a serving bowl and sprinkle with the chives or spring onion tops.

## KIDNEY BEAN AND BACON SALAD

This salad will keep for up to 3 days in the refrigerator.

*75 g (3 oz) streaky bacon, derinded*
*432 g (15¼ oz) can red kidney beans, drained*
*125 g (4 oz) frozen sweetcorn, cooked*
*4 spring onions, chopped*
*1 quantity Lemon and Honey Dressing**

**Serves 4**
**Preparation time:**
15 minutes

1. Grill the bacon on both sides until crisp and golden, drain on kitchen paper, then chop finely.
2. Place the bacon, kidney beans, sweetcorn and spring onions in a serving bowl, add the dressing and stir well.

## SUNSET SALAD

This salad is as delicious to eat as it is stunning to look at. The sweet orange slices are the perfect foil to the slightly bitter radicchio.

*few lettuce leaves*
*1 small radicchio*
*½ bunch radishes, sliced*
*125 g (4 oz) raw beetroot, grated*
*2 oranges*
*1 quantity French dressing**

**Serves 4**
**Preparation time:** 10 minutes

1. Arrange the lettuce leaves around the edge of a flat plate. Place the radicchio leaves in a circle inside the lettuce. Sprinkle the radishes over the lettuce.
2. Place the beetroot in the centre of the plate.
3. Peel the oranges and divide into segments, discarding all white pith and pips. Arrange the orange segments radiating from the centre of the plate.
4. Pour the dressing over the salad just before serving.

## HOT POTATO SALAD

*750 g (1½ lb) potatoes*
*7 tablespoons olive oil*
*4 rashers streaky bacon, derinded and chopped*
*2 celery sticks, chopped*
*2 cloves garlic, crushed*
*2 teaspoons Dijon mustard*
*2 tablespoons wine vinegar*
*salt and pepper to taste*
*few chopped celery leaves to garnish*

**Serves 4–6**
**Preparation time:** 25 minutes

1. Cut the potatoes into chunks, about 2.5 cm (1 inch). Cook in boiling salted water for about 15 minutes, until just tender. Drain well and place in a warmed serving dish.
2. Meanwhile, make the dressing. Heat 1 tablespoon of the oil in a frying pan, add the bacon and fry until crispy. Add the celery and garlic and cook gently for 5 minutes, until the celery is softened.
3. Stir in the remaining oil, the mustard and vinegar. Sprinkle with a little pepper and bring briefly to the boil.
4. Pour the dressing over the potatoes and sprinkle with celery leaves.

### VARIATION

Replace the bacon with 125 g (4 oz) sliced button mushrooms; fry in the oil until soft. Replace the celery with 1 cored, seeded and sliced red pepper.

## LETTUCE DRESSED WITH BUTTER

To ensure success, choose a good crispy lettuce for this salad and chill it well before serving.

*1 crispy lettuce, e.g. Cos or Webbs*
*2 teaspoons lemon juice*
*25 g (1 oz) butter, melted*
*salt and pepper to taste*

1. Tear the lettuce into large pieces. Shake off any excess water after washing and place the leaves in a large polythene bag. Chill for at least 1 hour.
2. Stir the lemon juice into the butter, season with a little salt and plenty of pepper and leave until lukewarm.
3. Place the lettuce in a serving bowl and pour over the butter, tossing lightly. Serve immediately.

**Serves 4**
**Preparation time:** 10 minutes, plus chilling time

## LEEK AND EGG SALAD

*250 g (8 oz) leeks, sliced thinly*
*½ Iceberg lettuce, shredded*
*2 hard-boiled eggs, chopped roughly*
*1 tablespoon capers, chopped*
*1 quantity French Dressing**
*1 tablespoon chopped parsley*

**Serves** 4–6
**Preparation time:** 20 minutes

1. Cook the leeks in boiling salted water for 2 minutes; drain and cool quickly under running cold water.
2. Cover the base of a salad bowl with the lettuce and pile the leeks on top. Sprinkle with the egg and capers.
3. Pour over the dressing; sprinkle with parsley to serve.

## CARROT AND CELERIAC SALAD

Early in the season when young turnips appear in the shops, try these instead of celeriac.

*350 g (12 oz) carrots, grated*
*350 g (12 oz) celeriac, grated*
*2 tablespoons chopped spring onion tops*
*1 clove garlic, crushed*
*1 quantity Lemon French Dressing**

**Serves** 4–6
**Preparation time:** 15 minutes

1. Arrange small piles of carrot and celeriac alternately around a flat plate. Sprinkle with the spring onion tops.
2. Add the garlic to the dressing. Pour evenly over the vegetables just before serving.

## WINTER ARTICHOKE SALAD

*750 g (1½ lb) Jerusalem artichokes*
*2 tablespoons lemon juice*
*2 cloves garlic, crushed*
*2 tablespoons olive oil*
*1 tablespoon chopped parsley*
*¼ teaspoon paprika*
*salt to taste*

**Serves** 4
**Preparation time:** 20 minutes
**Cooking time:** 12–15 minutes

1. Peel the artichokes and place immediately in a pan of cold water to which the lemon juice has been added. Boil for 12–15 minutes, until tender; drain and leave to cool.
2. Slice the artichokes thickly and place on a serving plate.
3. Mix together the garlic, oil, parsley and paprika. Drizzle over the artichokes and sprinkle with salt.

## SPICY MUSHROOMS

These mushrooms are good warm or cold and can be made up to 3 days in advance—the sauce is gradually absorbed by the mushrooms giving them a rich flavour.

*1 tablespoon oil*
*1 small onion*
*1 clove garlic, crushed*
*3 tablespoons wine vinegar*
*2 teaspoons Dijon mustard*
*2 tablespoons tomato purée*
*150 ml (1/4 pint) water*
*2 tablespoons dark brown soft sugar*
*2 teaspoons Worcestershire sauce*
*250 g (8 oz) button mushrooms*

**Serves** 4
**Preparation time:** 20 minutes

1. Heat the oil in a saucepan, add the onion and garlic and fry until softened. Add the remaining ingredients, except the mushrooms, and bring to the boil.
2. Reduce the heat and simmer for 10 minutes, stirring occasionally. Cut the mushrooms into quarters if large, and place in a bowl. Pour over the hot sauce and stir well.
3. Leave until the sauce is cold, stirring occasionally to ensure the mushrooms are evenly coated.
4. Serve with cold meats or grilled food.

## LETTUCE AND FLAGEOLET SALAD

For a quickly assembled salad, use a 432 g (15 oz) can flageolet beans—well drained—instead of dried beans.

*250 g (8 oz) flageolet beans, soaked overnight*
*1 quantity Herb French Dressing**
*1/2 crispy lettuce*
*1 tablespoon chopped mixed herbs (e.g. tarragon, chives, parsley)*

**Serves** 4
**Preparation time:** 10 minutes, plus soaking and standing time
**Cooking time:** 45–55 minutes

1. Drain the beans and rinse well. Place in a large saucepan with plenty of cold water and bring to the boil. Boil rapidly for 10 minutes, then simmer for 35–45 minutes, until tender but not mushy.
2. Drain the beans thoroughly, place in a bowl and pour over the dressing. Leave until cold; the warm beans will absorb most of the dressing.
3. Tear the lettuce into small pieces and place in a large serving bowl. Pile the beans on top and sprinkle with the chopped herbs to serve.

# BEETROOT AND CELERY SALAD

*350 g (12 oz) raw beetroot, grated*
*4 celery sticks, chopped finely*
*1 orange, segmented and chopped*
*1 quantity Parsley and Onion Dressing**
*celery leaves to garnish*

1. Place the beetroot, celery and orange in a serving bowl.
2. Add the dressing and mix well. Garnish with a few celery leaves.

**Serves 4–6**
**Preparation time:** 20 minutes

## CARIBBEAN FRUIT SALAD

*1 peach or guava*
*1 mango*
*2 bananas*
*2 slices fresh pineapple*
*2 tablespoons pineapple juice*
*1 tablespoon demerara sugar*
*1/4 teaspoon grated nutmeg*
*1/2 teaspoon ground cinnamon*
*2 tablespoons dark rum*

**Serves 4**
**Preparation time:**
10 minutes

1. Stone and chop the peach and mango into large chunks. Slice the bananas thickly. Core the pineapple and cut the flesh into large chunks.
2. Place all the fruit and the pineapple juice in a serving bowl and mix well.
3. Mix together the sugar and spices and sprinkle evenly over the fruit.
4. Warm the rum in a small pan, ignite it and pour over the fruit salad to serve.

## ICE MOUNTAIN FRUIT SALAD

The Chinese like to serve their fruit in bite-size pieces over a bed of ice. Use chopsticks for authenticity. Traditionally this fruit salad is served with tiny bowls of pink-tinted sugar, but sugar should not be needed if you choose a good selection of ripe fruits.

*1 kg (2 lb) mixed fresh fruit in season, e.g. cherries, pineapple, grapes, strawberries, satsumas, apples, kiwi fruit, lychees, kumquats, passion fruit, figs, etc.*
*plenty of ice cubes*

**Serves 4–6**
**Preparation time:**
15–20 minutes

1. Prepare the fruit as necessary: leave small fruit such as cherries and strawberries whole; segment citrus fruits; cut larger fruits into small chunks.
2. Just before serving, pile the ice onto a large serving plate and arrange the prepared fruit on top. Everyone helps themselves to fruits of their choice.

## WINTER FRUIT SALAD

This salad keeps well for up to a week in the refrigerator. Any dried fruits can be used.

*300 ml (½ pint) red wine*
*1 cinnamon stick*
*3 cloves*
*125 g (4 oz) raisins*
*125 g (4 oz) dried apricots, soaked if necessary*
*50 g (2 oz) dried prunes, soaked if necessary*
*2 firm cooking pears*
*2 clementines, segmented*
*25–50 g (1–2 oz) dark brown soft sugar*

**Serves 6**
**Preparation time:** 10 minutes, plus soaking time (if needed)
**Cooking time:** 30 minutes

1. Place the wine, cinnamon stick, cloves, raisins, apricots and prunes in a saucepan. Bring to the boil, then simmer for 15 minutes.
2. Peel, core and chop the pears, add to the pan and simmer for 10 minutes.
3. Add the clementines and stir well.
4. Add the sugar and cook for about 5 minutes, until slightly syrupy. Serve warm or cold, with natural fromage frais or yogurt.

## CINNAMON FRUIT SALAD

*125 g (4 oz) sugar*
*300 ml (½ pint) water*
*1 cinnamon stick*
*2 oranges*
*1 red dessert apple, chopped*
*1 pear, chopped*
*1 nectarine, stoned and chopped*
*125 g (4 oz) plums, stoned and chopped*
*125 g (4 oz) grapes, seeded*
*1 banana*

**Serves 6**
**Preparation time:** 30 minutes, plus cooling time

1. Place the sugar, water and cinnamon stick in a saucepan. Cut a thin sliver of rind from one of the oranges and add to the pan. Bring slowly to the boil, stirring to dissolve the sugar, then boil without stirring for 5 minutes, until the syrup is slightly thickened. Leave to cool slightly.
2. Peel the oranges, discarding all the rind and white pith. Cut down between the membranes to remove the segments, then chop each segment into 3 pieces, discarding any pips.
3. Place all the fruit, except the banana, in a bowl. Pour over the warm syrup, place a plate on top to keep the fruit submerged and leave to cool.
4. Just before serving, remove the cinnamon stick and orange rind. Slice the banana and add to the bowl.

# ORIENTAL FRUIT SALAD

If you like the flavour of ginger, add a little chopped stem ginger and 1 tablespoon of the syrup from the jar.

*2 oranges*
*1 small melon*
*2 kiwi fruit*
*425 g (15 oz) can lychees, drained*

1. Peel and segment the oranges over a bowl to catch the juice, discarding all pith.
2. Cut the melon in half, scoop out and discard the seeds. Remove the flesh with a melon baller or cut into small cubes. Slice the kiwi fruit thinly.
3. Place all the fruit in a serving bowl and add any orange juice. Chill for at least 2 hours before serving.

**Serves** 4
**Preparation time:** 20 minutes, plus chilling time

## MINTED STRAWBERRIES

*500 g (1 lb) strawberries*
*1 tablespoon chopped mint*
*2 tablespoons clear honey*
*2 tablespoons orange juice*

**Serves 4**
**Preparation time:** 10 minutes, plus marinating

1. Place the strawberries in a serving dish.
2. Blend together the mint, honey and orange juice until smooth, pour over the strawberries and leave to marinate at room temperature for 1 hour.
3. Serve with whipped cream or natural fromage frais.

## STRAWBERRY AND GRAPEFRUIT CUPS

Cassis brings out the strawberry flavour in the sauce and gives it a beautiful rich colour.

*2 grapefruit*
*500 g (1 lb) strawberries*
*2 tablespoons Cassis*

**Serves 4**
**Preparation time:** 15 minutes

1. Halve the grapefruit. Using a small sharp knife, cut between the membranes and around the edge to remove the fruit. Place the empty halves in 4 individual dishes.
2. Place the grapefruit segments in a bowl with two thirds of the strawberries and mix gently together. Divide between the grapefruit halves.
3. Place the remaining strawberries and the liqueur in a blender or food processor and work until smooth. Pour a little sauce over each grapefruit cup to serve.

## FRUIT SALAD VINAIGRETTE

This salad goes very well with strongly flavoured meat dishes, such as steak and game. It can either be served on a large platter or as a garnish to each plate of food.

*2 slices fresh pineapple*
*1 paw-paw, peeled*
*1 mango, peeled*
*2 bananas, sliced thinly*
*1 quantity French Dressing**

**Serves 4**
**Preparation time:** 20 minutes

1. Cut the edge of the pineapple slices into a zig-zag pattern, then cut each slice in half.
2. Cut the paw-paw in half and remove the seeds. Cut the paw-paw and mango lengthways into slices.
3. Arrange the fruit attractively on a serving plate and pour a little dressing over the top.